Coaching Advanced Soccer Players

by Richard Bate
technical director
soccer association of malaysia

published by
REEDSWAIN INC

Library of Congress Cataloging - in - Publication Data

Bate, Richard
   Coaching Advanced Soccer Players

ISBN No. 1-890946-33-8
Library of Congress Catalog Card Number 99-065727
Copyright © August 1999

Reedswain Books are available at special discounts for bulk purchase. For detail call the REEDSWAIN office at 1-800-331-5191.

Art Direction, Layout and Design
Kimberly N. Bender

Editing and Proofing
Bryan R. Beaver

Printed by
DATA REPRODUCTIONS
Auburn Hills Michigan

REEDSWAIN INC.
612 Pughtown Road
Spring City, PA 19475
1-800-331-5191
www.reedswain.com

introduction

This book is written as a handbook of practices that can be used by coaches working with high school and college players. The contents are practices that are workable, easily organized and effective training and coaching situations in which players can learn and develop their skills and understanding of the game.

Even with the minimum of input from the coach, players can develop their abilities through the design and nature of the practice. The coach however needs to organize and control the practice and direct the players' attention to the necessary skills to be developed. The major coaching points have been included in the text.

This book is designed to help any coach in the organization and presentation of his work and to further extend his knowledge of possible training ideas. By using this book as a reference, the coach through modifications and adjustments can devise new but similar practices with a different learning emphasis and so extend the range of his players' abilities.

At all times players should be encouraged to play realistically and at match pace whenever possible. Attacking players, defenders and goalkeepers should perform in practice with the same intensity, desire, quality and thought as the coach would expect in match play. If players have difficulty in practices because they are placed under too much pressure, then the coach should reduce numbers, increase playing areas or modify the practice situation to suit the needs of the players.

The author has found all the enclosed practices to be extremely effective in the teaching and development of game skills and understanding.

contents

index

"Neutral" players referred to in this book are players who assist or play for both teams. They play with and under the same rules as the team in possession. Unless otherwise specified they never defend!

Goals are always full size unless otherwise indicated in the practice organization.

Legend

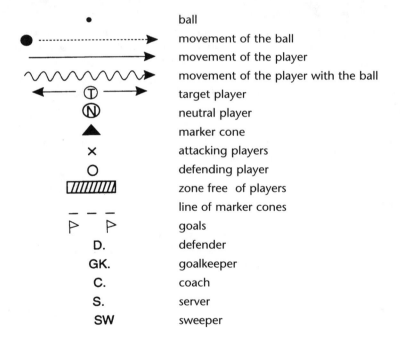

•	ball
	movement of the ball
	movement of the player
	movement of the player with the ball
Ⓣ	target player
Ⓝ	neutral player
▲	marker cone
×	attacking players
○	defending player
▨▨▨	zone free of players
	line of marker cones
⊳ ⊳	goals
D.	defender
GK.	goalkeeper
C.	coach
S.	server
SW	sweeper

playing area	players involved
1. 20 yards x 20 yards square	5 attackers 2 defenders
equipment 1. 5 red bibs/shirts 2. 2 white bibs/shirts	**practice rules** 1. 5 attackers attempt to record 10 passes 2. No restrictions on the number of touches 3. 2 defenders win possession three times and replace 2 attackers

coach's notes

This is a simple possession practice where players develop their skills of passing and supporting each other. Players in possession should try to pass to teammates, especially those behind opponents and to play to their feet, accurately and with not too much pace on the pass (easy enough for the receiver to play a one touch pass if needed.) Simple, early passes should be delivered and after having delivered the pass, players should adjust their positions so as to receive a return pass if necessary.

When supporting the man in possession, players should find positions where the ball can be passed to their feet without a chance of interception by any of the defenders, and continually need to find new support positions within the playing area as the ball changes position. Spreading-out in the playing area helps to create space and therefore time for the attacking team.

ALL players at ALL times should see everything around them - positions of teammates, position and opponents, lines on the field etc. As the play improves then possibly one or two of the attackers could be restricted to 1 touch passing only and eventually all attackers could be restricted to using one touch whenever possible.

Particularly useful as an introductory practice or warm-up before major coaching sessions.

practice no. 1

Purpose
passing skills and possession

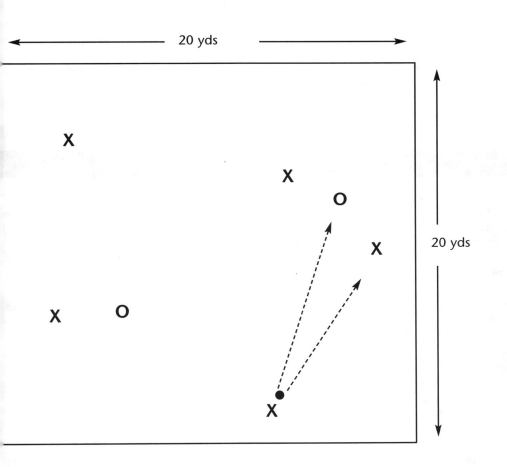

playing area	players involved
1. 60 yards x 40 yards	5 attackers 2 defenders

equipment	practice rules
1. 6 red bibs/shirts 2. 6 white bibs/shirts 3. 2 neutral colors 4. A supply of balls around the field.	1. No restrictions on touches of the ball 2. Score 1 point for each individual pass made 3. Goal is to score 20 points

coach's notes

A similar practice to 5 v 2 in that players continually think and work on passing movement and supporting each other. However, in this practice two neutral players are included and always play for the team in possession of the ball - they never defend. In this much larger practice of 60 x 40 yards players are virtually playing on a quarter of a soccer field. Numbers of players involved are larger, and so more options are available to players both in possession and when supporting.

Six red-shirted players and the two neutral players should pass and move to keep possession of the ball using the whole playing area. In possession, players should discipline themselves to pass accurately and carefully and must decide whether to pass to feet, to spaces, along the ground or in the air. Off the ball, players should be looking for positions and spaces away from opponents if possible in order to receive passes and once again, spreading out to use the whole playing area will help the team in possession. Players can develop the skills of passing to marked players (i.e. to the side furthest away from the defender so that the ball may be screened or protected if necessary) and also long-passes over fifty yards or so.

If possession is lost, then that team becomes the defending team and must work to regain possession quickly. Normal rules apply and if the ball goes out of play over any line, then the practice is restarted with a throw-in. Once again, 1 touch passing can be encouraged and also wall-passes (1 - 2 's) can be used to defeat opponents in congested areas.

practice no. 2

Purpose
passing skills and possession

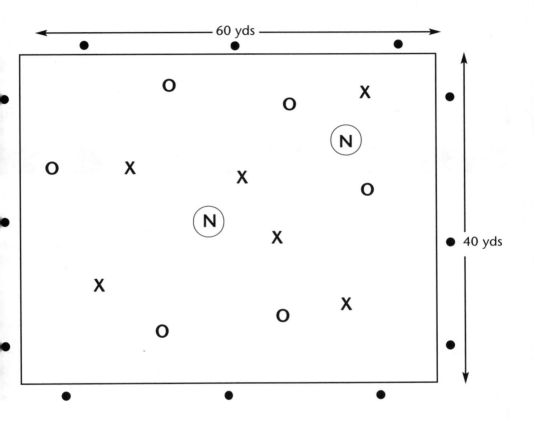

playing area 1. Half a soccer field 2. 2 x 5 yards end zones	**players involved: - 18** 1. 2 teams of 8 players 2. 2 neutral players
equipment 1. 8 red bibs/shirts 2. 8 white bibs/shirts 3. 2 neutral colors 4. 3 or 4 balls	**practice rules** 1. Play 8 v 8 and include 2 neutral players when in possession 2. A point is scored when a receiving player puts his foot on the ball in the end zone 3. Throw-in for the ball over side-lines

coach's notes

A further progression in practice in that the total area is larger and numbers have also increased. However a further dimension has been added to the play in that 'direction' has been added to possession. On gaining possession of the ball each team must retain possession and attempt to move the ball into the opponent's end zone and one player must put his foot on the ball in that zone. The practice again includes 2 neutral players. If a team is successful the opponents gain possession and attempt to score in the other end zone, so play is end to end.

Players now must use all their passing and supporting skills to progress the ball towards their opponent's defensive area. Forward passing if possible and the elimination of unnecessary back and square passes should be encouraged. Support positions ahead of the ball and behind opponents should be sorted out and all thought should be concerned with moving the ball forward quickly, accurately and economically into the opponent's end zone.

Players must now incorporate a variety of passing skills - long, short, ground, aerial, through passes, wall-passes and employ whichever skill is necessary to advance the ball quickly and accurately.

On gaining possession, quick counter-attacks can be initiated by a quick release of passes or by running the ball forward if space exists. All in all, this is an enjoyable, flowing practice that can benefit all players in passing, supporting and general attacking skills and also in their defending priorities.

practice no. 3

Purpose
passing skill and possession

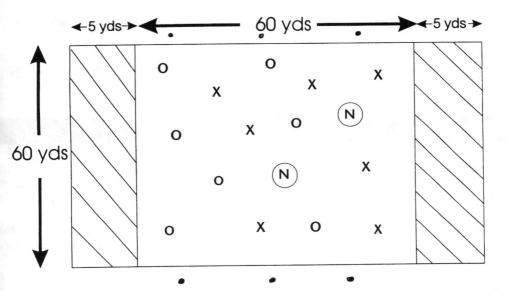

playing area	**players involved: - 16**
1. 70 yards x 40 yards area	1. 2 teams of 6
2. 2 end zones of 5 yards in length	2. 2 neutral players
	3. 2 target players

equipment	**practice rules**
1. 6 red bibs/shirts	1. Two teams of 6 play against each other and include 2 neutrals when in possession.
2. 6 white bibs/shirts	
3. 2 neutral colors	
4. 2 blue bibs/shirts for 'Targets'	2. Play to pass ball to (T) behind line. Receive ball back from (T) and pass to (T) at other end of the field.

coach's notes

Objectives here are similar to the previous practice in that to be successful, a team must use its possession to reach a target behind the opponent's goal-line. So once more, direction and attacking purpose is added to ability to retain possession.

Two neutral players play for the team in possession and two target players are stationed behind the end lines. The team in possession should attempt to play to the target player who is mobile behind the end lines. If they are successful, then they retain possession and attack to pass the ball to the target player at the opposite end. They retain possession and attempt to play to each target player in turn. On gaining possession, opponents can pass to either target and then must attack the opposite end.

Opportunities exist here to use long forward passes to the target player who cannot use his hands on receiving passes and must control the ball inside the end lines before returning it to the team from whom he received the ball.

This drill requires all skills involved in passing and support. Running with the ball should be encouraged and obviously more players and an increased playing area can be used if necessary.

practice no. 4

Purpose
passing and possession

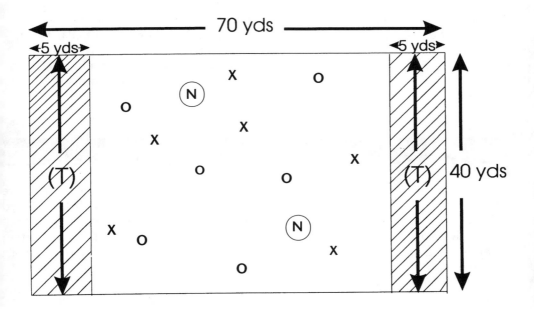

playing area	players involved: - 14
1. 50 yards x 30 yards	1. 10 attacking players
	2. 4 defending players

equipment	practice rules
1. 10 red bibs/shirts	1. 5 v 2 in 20 yds x 30 yds area
2. 4 white bibs/shirts	2. When opportunity arises, use a long pass to switch the play to far zone.
3. Supply of balls	3. Two defenders from mid zone enter to defend and other 2 rest in middle zone

coach's notes

In this practice both short-range passing and support and long-range passing are developed. Five attackers retain possession against two defenders in a 20 yd x 30 yd zone. Given the opportunity, a player in possession should transfer the ball by using a long, driven or lofted pass to the five players in the other end zone. Two resting defenders in the middle zone move to oppose the five who receive the long pass while the other two defenders move into the central zone to rest.

By nominating 'one' player to receive the long pass, a greater emphasis on accuracy of delivery is required by the man in possession. Players should concentrate on retaining possession by good quality passing, support and movement.

Players should look for the opportunity to switch the play to the other zone as they play possession soccer. Their first controlling touch should move the ball into a position that makes for easy delivery of the long pass. Players must concentrate on retaining possession while looking for the chance to deliver the long pass with accuracy.

practice no. 5

Purpose
possession and long passing

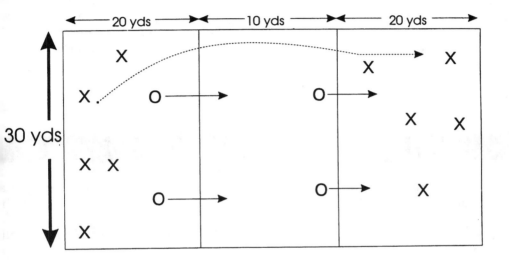

playing area	**players involved: - 14**
1. 60 yards x 40 yards	1. 2 teams of 6
	2. 2 goalkeepers

equipment	**practice rules**
1. 6 red bibs/shirts	1. If a goal is scored, that team must,
2. 6 white bibs/shirts	on gaining possession again, play
3. 2 goalkeeper jerseys	possession - soccer and cannot
4. 2 portable goals	score until opponents have
5. Supply of balls	equalized.

coach's notes

This practice encourages both passing, support and movement and pressurizing as a defending ploy.

Once a goal has been scored by either team, that same team cannot score again until the opponents have equalized. The team must, on gaining possession play "keep-away," retaining possession of the ball being their sole purpose. The team who has conceded the goal should pressurize vigorously to regain possession in order to score an equalizing goal. On an equalizing goal being scored, the game returns to normal and once again teams play to score past their opponent's goalkeeper.

practice no. 6

Purpose
possession and pressurizing

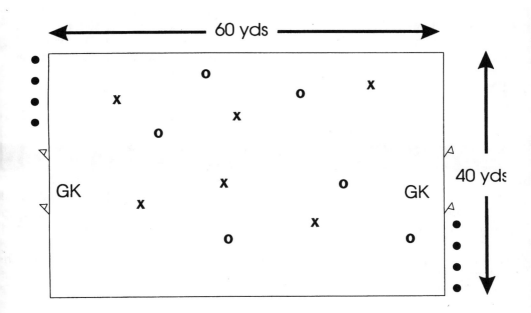

playing area	players involved: - 14
1. 60 yards x 30 yards wide	1. 2 teams of 6
2. 3 zones of 20 yards length by 30 yards width.	2. 2 goalkeepers

equipment	practice rules
1. 10 red bibs/shirts	1. No restrictions on touches on ball
2. 5 white bibs/shirts	2. X's in possession should play 5 v 2
3. 3 or 4 balls	to use a wall-pass to run with the ball into the middle zone and play 2 v 1 in middle zone so as to run the ball into the end zone to make 5 v 2.

coach's notes

This practice enables players to develop shorter-range passing skills, especially wall passes and skills of running with the ball. The 5 x's should keep possession and attempt to use a wall pass or wall-passes to enable one player to run with the ball into the middle zone, the player should combine with his fellow attacker if necessary (possibly by playing a wall-pass) to produce the situation to run with the ball into the end zone where the ball must be passed to x10 behind the end line. The five players now in that zone repeat the process in order to run the ball back to the original zone.

On playing wall-passes the man in possession must release the pass to the wall from approximately 3 - 4 yards away from the defender. The pass should be played accurately to the feet of the wall-player and at the correct pace (certainly not too hard) before the passer accelerates past the defender to receive the return pass. Occasionally the pass can be played to the space around the foot (of the wall) furthest away from the defender. The wall player should find a position where he can receive the pass with no chance of interception by the defender. The distance of the wall player should be around 4 - 5 yards from the defender, certainly not too far as wall passes should be executed quickly before defenders can recover against the move. The return pass from the wall to the runner should be played one-touch if possible and into the space ahead of the running player.

So, in this practice, short-range passing, movement, wall-passes and running with the ball can all be developed and it is a practice full of good soccer, momentum and game situations.

practice no. 7

Purpose
wall-passes

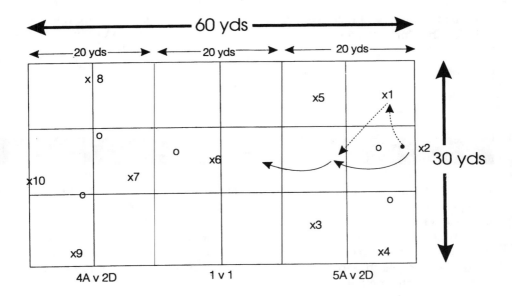

playing area	players involved: - 9/10
1. Quarter of a soccer field (60 yards) x 40 yards	1. 2 goalkeepers 2. 2 "wall" players - (T1) and (T2) 3. 1 defender 4. 4/5 attackers
equipment 1. 2 portable goals 2. Plentiful supply of balls 3. Bib/shirt for defender	**practice rules** 1. Players should run with the ball, play a wall-pass movement with (T2) and then a wall-pass movement with (T1) and receive to score past either goalkeeper.

coach's notes

One method of eliminating opponents in the central areas in front of goal is by usin wall-passes. Wall-passes can be best employed when defenders are within 3 - 4 yard of the man in possession, and the attacker has forward momentum and a suppo player to employ for the wall-pass. In this practice, the man in possession has momer tum by carrying the ball forward at the defender. On approaching his opponent, h should choose whether to use a wall-pass to bypass him or to feint to play a wall-pas and run on with the ball. The pass from the player in possession can be to feet, bu the return player mush decide which goalkeeper to attack and how to beat him.

practice no. 8

urpose
vall-passes and shooting

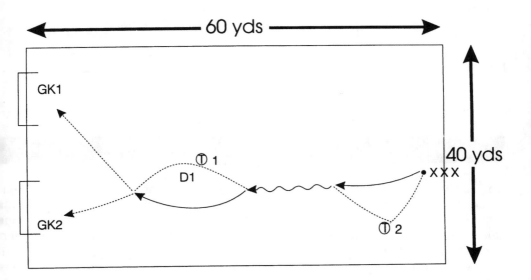

playing area	players involved: - 9/10
1. 40 yards x 40 yards	1. 3 teams of 5 players each team

equipment	practice rules
1. 3 sets of different colored bibs/shirts. 2. Supply of balls.	1. 2 of 3 teams play 2 touch soccer against each other and may use neutral player in the playing area and the 4 neutral players outside the area to do so. 2. All players inside the area have a maximum of 2 touches of the ball in their possession.

coach's notes

The ability to use quick passing and take the minimum number of touches on the ball when in possession is the hall-mark of great players and great teams. The fact that the ball can move quicker than opponents means that any team capable of playing high quality one or two touch soccer can destroy opposition defenses quickly and effectively. Players should have regular practice in quick 1 touch and 2 touch passing. This practice almost ensures that any player receiving the ball has options to pass to. Players in his team inside the playing area and the neutral player should consistently move into receiving positions so that early 1 or 2 touch passes can be delivered. Players outside the playing area can move anywhere along their lines and can have as many touches as they feel necessary, but try to use 1 or 2 if possible. Should one team totally dominate the play by scoring say 20 consecutive passes then all 3 teams of 5 should change functions, each team alternating as neutral players who return the ball to whichever team they received it from.

practice no. 9

<u>Purpose</u>
quick passing and movement

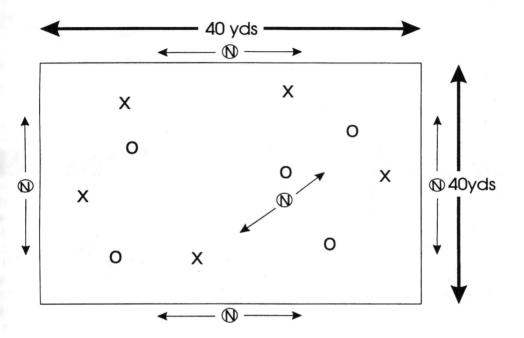

playing area	players involved: - 13
1. 60 yards x 30 yards	1. 5 v 2 in one zone
2. 3 zones of 20 yards x 30 yards	2. 4 v 2 in one zone
equipment	**practice rules**
1. 9 red shirts/bibs	1. 5 v 2 in end zone until one player creates the opportunity to run with the ball out of the zone, through the middle zone and into the other end zone to release a pass to the player behind the end line. Now repeat, moving in the other direction.
2. 4 white shirts/bibs	
3. Cones to mark zones	
4. Supply of balls	
	2. Any attacking player may run the ball out of the zone when in possession.

coach's notes

Soccer is not just a passing game. Running with the ball is a very effective method of moving forward in possession towards the opponent's goal. Running with the ball involves covering the ground as quickly as possible while retaining control of the ball. It can be used to make ground quickly in any direction: towards goal, away from opponents and perhaps has more certainty of possession than passing when carried out efficiently. It is particularly useful for flank players such as full-backs and wingers and also for midfield players breaking forward at opponents. Players should push the ball forward in front of their body in order to run quickly almost in a 'push and chase' the ball manner while keeping their head up wherever possible. The practice above helps players to develop this ability to run with the ball and is a useful introductory activity at the start of a practice session, following the initial warm-up. Players should be encouraged to pass, support and look for the chance to 'run' the ball forward whenever possible. Of course, by running the ball, possibilities for wall-passes and 'dummy' to pass while retaining possession become a part of this practice.

practice no. 10

Purpose
Running with the ball

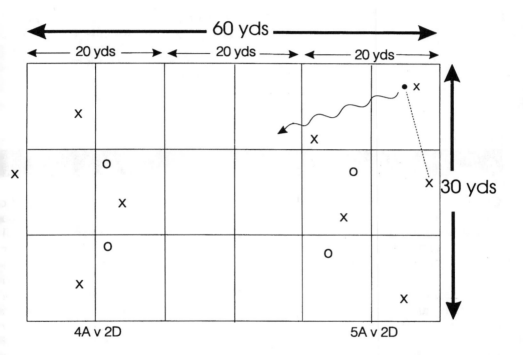

4A v 2D   5A v 2D

playing area	players involved: - 7
1. 44 yards wide	1. 6 attacking players
2. Half-a-pitch length	2. 1 goalkeepers

equipment	practice rules
1. 1 ball for each player 2. 1 goal 3. Extra supply of balls in a semi circle	1. Attacker on coaches command runs with his ball towards the penalty area. 2. On entering the penalty area he must attempt to score 1 v 1 past the goalkeeper before turning and sprinting quickly back to the half-way line.

coach's notes

Often in a game, players break free of a defense and are then faced with a 1 v 1 situation with the goalkeeper. In this practice, attackers should move quickly with the ball at their feet, using the minimum number of touches to reach the penalty area. On entering the penalty area, the attacker should attempt to score in a 1 v 1 with the goalkeeper, either by shooting or dribbling past the goalkeeper.

As soon as the result of his attempt at goal scoring is known, the second man in his team runs quickly with his ball from the semi-circle around the half-way line and attempts to score in the 1 v 1 with the goal keeper. This sequence is repeated until minute (or even 2 minutes) has elapsed and the number of goals scored by the six attackers is recorded.

A second team of six now attempts to beat the score and in this way, a competitive element is introduced into the practice both for individual players and for the two competing teams trying to score.

practice no. 11

Jnning with the ball and 1 v 1 with the goalkeeper

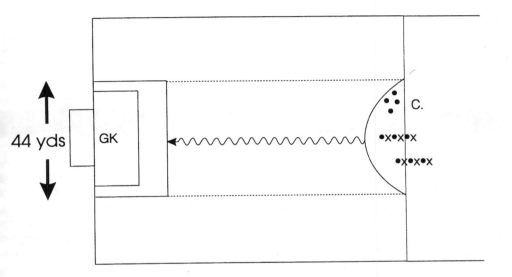

playing area	players involved: - 18
1. 30 yards long x 44 yards wide	1. 2 goalkeepers
2. A penalty area, extended by 12 yds.	2. 4 servers
	3. 12 strikers

equipment	practice rules
1. Portable goals	1. X3 and X4 make quick direct runs into the penalty area to strike at goal
2. Marker cones	2. As they commence their runs, X1 crosses the ball into their path for the strike at goal.
3. Plentiful supply of balls	3. Repeat, moving in other direction and crosses from X2 are played for X5 and X6.

coach's notes

One-third of all goals scored originate from a cross, and that is a massive source of goals by any standard. Consequently, crossing and finishing at goal should be a regular part of any team's practice sessions - some would say in every practice session. Crosses should be played beyond the reach of the goalkeeper. The area between the penalty spot and goal line is a particularly fruitful area from which goals are scored from crosses. Should it not be possible to deliver the ball into this area because defenders occupy it, then crosses beyond the far-post area also produce many goals and goal creating opportunities. In this practice, the crossers need employ only 2 touches on the ball. The first touch should be to play the ball 4 - 5 yards forward and the second touch on the ball should be the actual delivery of the cross into the target areas mentioned. If the cross is played with pace and spin, this can create problems for any defenders and goalkeeper and can assist the attacking players greatly. The strikers should move quickly into the areas at the near-post and far-post and attempt to score with one touch of the ball, concentrating on keeping the ball low.

In this practice, players can work to score past both goalkeepers as service can be supplied by both x1 and x2. After attacking one goalkeeper, players can work in the other direction receiving a service from whichever server is appropriate. Obviously players can receive crosses from both left and right if the practice structure is altered.

practice no. 12

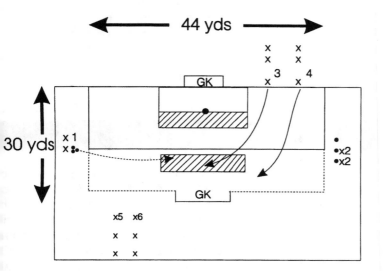

= target area for crosses

playing area	**players involved: - 14**
1. Half a soccer field - 60 yds in length	1. 4 attackers
2. 10 yards wide channel between penalty area line and touchline.	2. 4 defenders
	3. 4 wingers
	4. 2 goalkeepers

equipment	**practice rules**
1. 6 red shirts/bibs	1. GK delivers the ball to W playing for his team.
2. 6 white shirts/bibs	2. 'W' crosses ball to two strikers to attack ball to score.
3. 2 goalkeepers	3. If passes are intercepted, whichever team has possession pass to their winger to cross to strikers.
4. 1 portable goal	

coach's notes

In this practice, players will develop the ability to deliver crosses and to score from those crosses. The wingers ('W') should stay outside the playing are and receive passes from players of their team. On receiving passes the winger should either cross the ball quickly, or run with the ball before crossing into the goal scoring area. These strikers should be aware of where the goal scoring area is and how they may move into the area. Crosses should be delivered so that the goalkeeper cannot intercept the cross and strikers should attempt to lose their defenders with the change of pace and direction before attacking the cross to score. If the strikers move initially behind the marker it will be difficult for that defending player to see both the ball and him. From the position behind, or out of sight of the defender, the striker can decide whether to move quickly to a position in front of his opponent, or stay behind him for a cross delivered over his head. On striking at goal, the attackers should attempt to score with one touch and try to keep the ball low. Heading the ball, and particularly diving-headers and volleys are the skills most often used in scoring goals form crosses.

This is a flowing practice, from end to end, and is an exciting practice with many crosses, shots, and rebounds off the goalkeeper occurring. This brings enjoyment and excitement to a practice that will develop abilities in perhaps the most important of all skills, that of scoring goals, especially from crosses.

The practice may be further developed by introducing two midfield players to each team who look to break forward into the scoring areas to strike at goal, or look for headed clearances from defenders which lead to midfield players shooting or passing the ball wide, for the winger to cross once again.

practice no. 13

urpose
rossing the ball

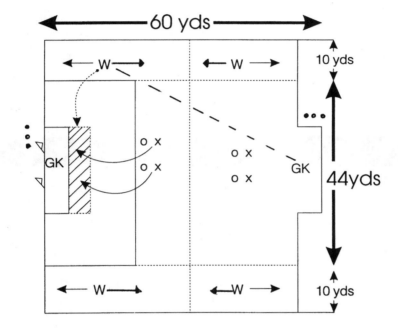

playing area	**players involved: - 14**
1. Area 40 yds x 36 yds long 2. Distance along goal-line = 20 yards	1. Two teams of 6 players 2. 2 goalkeepers 3. 4 players on one half - 2 in other as shown.
equipment	**practice rules :-**
1. 2 portable goals 2. 6 red shirts/bibs 3. 6 white shirts/bibs 4. 2 GK's jerseys 4. Supply of balls	1. Players must remain in allocated areas of play as shown 2. Ball out of play/over bar - game restarts by throw from GK in half where ball leaves play. Throws to own team

coach's notes

A free-flowing and enjoyable shooting practice for players is illustrated here. The playing area is nearly a double penalty area in that is 36 yards long and 40 yards wide a its widest point. The goalkeeper serves the ball by using his hands into any one of the four players in his team in the half nearest to his goal. They then play against the 2 challenging attacking players from the opposite team until a shot can be taken at the opposition goal. The two attacking players in each half should look to pick up any rebounds off the goalkeeper. The practice is end to end with each goalkeeper serving the ball after a shot has been saved or has missed the target at his end. Players should be encouraged to shoot at each and every opportunity and not to hesitate to strike form 20 - 25 yards. Keeping the ball low is of great importance and "hitting the target" goes without saying. Low shots travelling across the goalkeeper will cause him great difficulty and can provide secondary scoring chances if the goalkeeper does no hold the shot. Seeing the position of the goalkeeper will help considerably in deciding where to shoot. Other goalkeepers position themselves incorrectly and strikers can take advantage of this if they observe the errors and place shots as well as striking powerfully.

The practice is exciting and involves players continually moving, readjusting positions supporting each other to receive passes and shooting at any opportunity. Scoring from long-range (18 - 30 yards) requires controlled power and good technique and players should concentrate on keeping the ball low and "try to score." Too many player shoot recklessly and are only satisfied in making contact with the ball. Players must strike confidently and with a determination and desire to score with a cleanly struck powerful shot.

practice no. 14

Purpose
Long range shooting

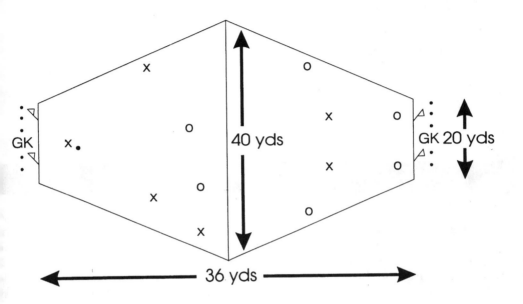

playing area	**players involved: - 14**
1. 30 yds x 25 yds	1. 6 attacking players
	2. 6 defenders
	3. 2 GK's

equipment	**practice rules :-**
1. 2 portable goals	1. GK1 throws the ball ahead of X1
2. 6 red shirts/bibs	who is the attacking player. He
3. 6 white shirts/bibs	moves forward onto the ball and
4. 2 GK's shirts	runs towards GK2. Defender O1
4. Cones	chases X1 to pressure him. X1
	under pressure attempts to score
	1 v 1 past the goalkeeper.

coach's notes

One of the most difficult situations in which a player can find himself is in a 1 v 1 with a goalkeeper. To score looks easier than it really is. In 1 v 1 situations, it is important for the striker to know two things of major importance. He needs to know how much time he has available to execute his shot and also the position of the goalkeeper as he advances. Observing the goalkeeper's position is easier than knowing how much time is available in which to work. Goalkeepers will make errors of judgment in their positioning and strikers should take advantage of this by placing their shot in any obvious spaces made available by a goalkeeper's mistake. The ball should be kept low and be punched firmly past the goalkeeper. If the goalkeeper's positioning is correct and he presents a difficult target to beat, the advancing attacker should move to within 5 - 6 yards of the goalkeeper and "pass" the ball past the goalkeeper keeping the ball low. Only 1 or 2 yards of space will be available at either side of the goalkeeper's feet through which to "pass" the ball, but the ball should be contacted firmly, confidently and through the center line. The attacker should place the ball to either side of the goalkeeper depending on which space appears more obvious. If the striker can deceive the goalkeeper before releasing his shot, then he should. 'Feinting' to shoot in one corner by shaping the body and head to do so can be followed by a shot into the opposite corner of the net.

practice no. 15

Purpose

scoring in 1 v 1 with the goalkeeper

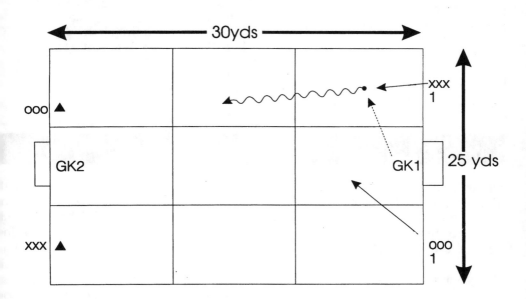

playing area	**players involved: - 14**
1. 30 yds x 25 yds	1. 2 goalkeepers 2. 2 teams of 6 numbered 1-6
equipment 1. 6 red shirts/bibs 2. 6 white shirts/bibs 3. 2 goalkeepers jerseys 4. 2 portable goals 5. Plentiful supply of balls	**practice rules:-** 1. Two teams of 6 are numbered 1-6 and whichever number is called by the coach, two players, one from each team, run from behind their goal to play 1 v 1 against each other to score past the opposing goalkeeper.

coach's notes

Opposing teams face each other over a playing area of 30 yards long by 25 yards wide. The coach is positioned outside the playing area and has a plentiful supply of soccer balls at his disposal. The coach calls out a number - say 5 - and both number fives, one from each team, sprint from behind their goal-line to try to be the first to a ball played into the playing area by the coach.

On gaining possession a player should attempt to score past his opponent's goalkeeper, either by dribbling past his opponent or shooting directly at goal on gaining possession. The practice continues until a goal is scored, or the ball leaves the playing area. If the ball rebounds from the goalkeeper after a shot, the practice continues. Players then retire from the practice area after their game is ended. The coach then calls out another number and two more players enter the field of play.

The coach could also call out two numbers to play together to score, and can also deliver a variety of services into the playing area for players to contest before attempting to score.

This is a very competitive and exiting practice enjoyed by all players and develops 1 v 1 ability in both attacking and defending skills as well as goalkeeping and of course shooting.

practice no. 16

Purpose
Shooting

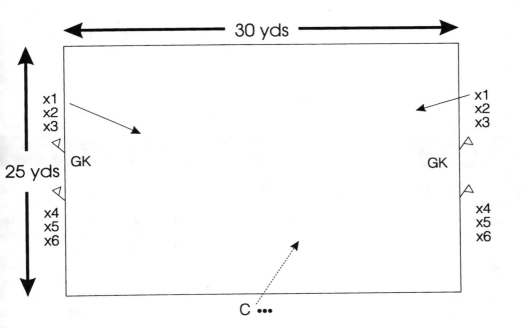

playing area 1. 36 yds long x 25 yds wide	**players involved: - 14** 1. 2 goalkeepers 2. 2 teams of 6 numbered 1-6

equipment
1. 2 portable goals
2. 1 ball for each attacking player
	practice rules:-
	1. X1 passes to O1 who is 10 yards away.
	2. O1 returns the ball first time to X1 and defends in the attacking half
	3. X1 runs the ball at O1 and
	  a) dribbles past O1 to shoot at goal
	  b) plays a wall-pass with (T) to shoot

coach's notes

A combined passing, running with the ball, wall-passing and shooting practice. X1 or passing to and receiving a return pass from O1 should attack with the ball. He car dribble past O1 or combine with (T) (who can move as needed to support X1) to play a wall-pass before shooting. O1 should be encouraged to pressurize and win posses sion in the attacking half and can actually be prevented by the coach from moving back over the half-way line in his defending role. When shooting, X1 should remem ber to shoot low across the goalkeeper and rebound his own shooting chance Defenders can also be introduced to chase X1 after he has received possession from O1, so that he must attack and shoot quickly before being caught by the recovering defender.

practice no. 17

Purpose
Shooting

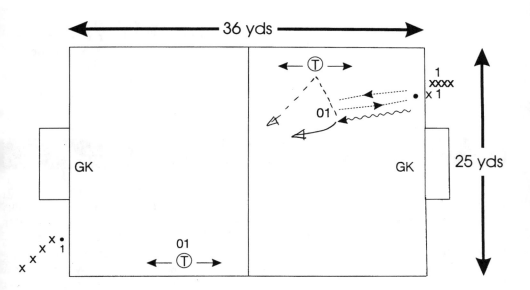

playing area 1. 40 yds long x 30 yds wide	**players involved: - 14** 1. 2 goalkeepers 2. 2 teams of 6 numbered 1-6
equipment 1. 2 full size goals 2. Supply of balls 3. 8 red shirts/bibs 4. 8 white shirts/bibs 5. 2 goalkeeper's jerseys	**practice rules:-** 1. GK serves the ball into his own team. 2. The team plays to score past the opponents' goalkeeper but can use the 4 players along the end line to assist by setting up shots for oncoming attackers.

coach's notes

In crowded penalty areas, players often need support in order to create shooting chances. The presence of supporting players enables strikers to play wall-passes, feint to pass to support players but retain possession and generally combine in quick inter-play to create scoring opportunities. The practice detailed here allows strikers to shoot using individual ability in creating the chance to score. Attackers should be encouraged to shoot at every opportunity, striking the ball powerfully and low from longer distances and 'place' the ball past the goalkeeper form distances much nearer. Composure, observing the goalkeeper's position before striking the ball and concentrating on precise technique should be encouraged by the coach as well as developing the players' ability to combine with other players to create scoring chances. The support players along the end line may be given only one touch to ' set' the ball to an oncoming striker, or he may be allowed a maximum of 3 touches according to the decision of the coach.

Players should take care with the passes they make to the target men so that a pass can be returned comfortably in order to set up a scoring opportunity.

After scoring a pre-determined number of goals, the teams can change roles and other players may then work. Those moving to a position behind the end line may now rest while still remaining alert and contributing to their team's performance as their team mates work to score goals in this practice.

practice no. 18

Purpose
Shooting

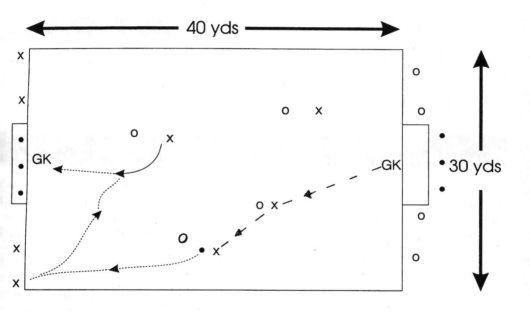

playing area	**players involved: - 15**
1. 44 yds long x 36 yds wide	1. 12 players
	2. 3 goalkeepers

equipment	**practice rules:-**
1. One fixed goal	1. Two teams of 6 score in any of the three goals within the area.
2. Two portable goals	2. On the scoring of a goal, the server delivers another ball into the playing area.
3. Supply of balls	3. First team to score 5 goals wins the competition.
4. 6 red shirts/bibs	
5. 6 white shirts/bibs	
5. 3 goalkeeper's jerseys	

coach's notes

The practice above gives players the opportunity to practice a variety of skills related to shooting at goal. Controlling the ball, volleying, power shooting, 1 v 1 situations with the goalkeeper will all arise in the course of this practice. It is an excellent practice also for goalkeepers. They must be constantly alert and can be involved at any time during the practice as teams may change the direction in which they are playing to suit their needs.

It is a quick, exciting shooting practice and obviously a plentiful supply of balls is necessary for the practice to function correctly. A playing session of either 5 minutes or the first team to score 5 goals can be the target for the players concerned.

practice no. 19

Purpose
shooting

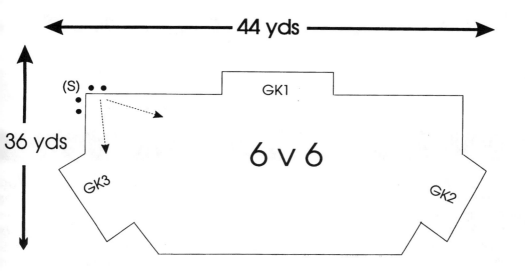

playing area	players involved: - 14
1. Extended goal-area to edge to edge of the penalty box. 2. 20 yards wide x 18 yards long	1. 1 server 2. 1 goalkeeper 3. 2 groups of 3 v 3 strikers
equipment 1. Marker cones to extend goal-area 2. Bibs and shirts to distinguish teams 3. Supply of balls	**practice rules:-** 1. (S) serves a variety of balls into the penalty box - ground/aerial. 2. Team gaining possession attempts to score. Other team defends.

coach's notes

This practice is a quick-fire, fast-moving practice that requires players to shoot almost immediately on receiving differing kinds of service. Balls should be served into the playing area at random by the coach, at a variety of heights and speeds. Players who gain possession should attempt to shoot, or combine with their teammates to score against the other three players who act as defenders. Whichever team gains possession becomes the attacking team and the others defend. As a variation, the team in possession could use resting players in the outside of the playing area to combine with in order to score, but players outside may not shoot - they can only 'feed' the attacking team. A good practice also for goalkeepers. If the ball leaves the playing area for any reason, the coach should quickly serve another ball. Two minutes can be allowed for this practice or a competition to decide which team is more successful from say 10 soccer balls served into the practice area. Keep a good supply of soccer balls handy!!

practice no. 20

Purpose
quick - shooting

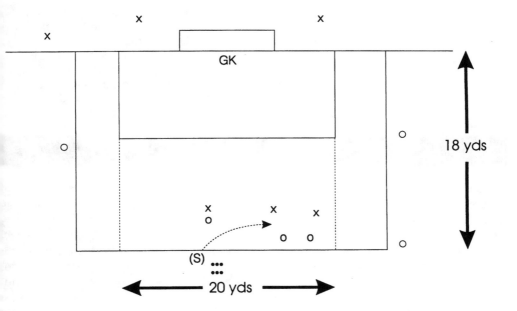

playing area	players involved: - 12
1. 50 yards wide x 40 yards long	1. 6 attackers 2. 5 defenders + 1 resting defender
equipment 1. 6 red shirts/bibs 2. 6 white shirts/bibs 3. Marker cones 3. Supply of balls	**practice rules:-** 1. Six attackers keep possession of the ball for as long as possible (max: 2 minutes) 2. Five defenders pressure, mark and challenge to force the ball out of the playing area. 3. Each time the ball is played outside the playing area by the defenders, a point is registered for them and a new ball is quickly served into the area to the attacking team.

coach's notes

Pressurizing is the skill or tactic of preventing your immediate opponent from playing leisurely when in possession. 'Pressurizing' aims at minimizing the time and space available for the attacking player. By physically moving into a position 2 or 3 yards away from the man in possession and threatening to dispossess him, this often has the effect of causing the opposition to play hurriedly and make mistakes. Pressurizing players must 'close-down' on their opponent in possession and literally try to force mistakes by threatening to challenge for the ball in a balanced and well-timed manner so as not to be beaten easily. Aggression, determination and quick feet are necessary to pressurize successfully on an individual basis, as well as lowering the body position and concentrating solely on the movement of the ball. Other defenders should attempt to intercept passes wherever possible. Pressurizing, to be successful, must be understood by all players as their role as pressurizing player or marker will quickly change in this practice situation. It should be a team effort and no player should be excused the running and working aspect of this tactic.

Each session of pressurizing in this practice lasts for a duration of 2 minutes and the resting defender must count the number of occasions his team forces the ball out of play in the time allotted. At the end of 2 minutes, the defending team becomes the attacking team with the resting defender becoming the sixth player. One of the attacking team now becomes a resting defender. The practice continues until all players have had a resting period outside of practice. At the end of the session, a grand total of successes can be calculated by adding up the count of each resting defender to find the winning team.

practice no. 21

Purpose
pressuring

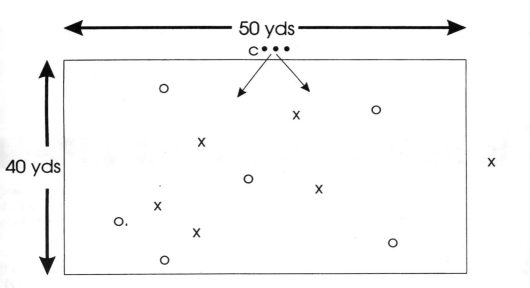

playing area	players involved: - 12
1. 40 yards long x 25 yards wide	1. 2 goalkeepers
	2. 1 server
	3. Attackers
	4. Defenders
equipment	**practice rules:-**
1. 2 portable goals	1. S (server) passes long to O1 behind the end line. (GK could also throw the ball)
2. Supply of balls	2. As soon as the ball passes over the half way line, X1 comes out to defend against O1.
	3. O1 attempts to score past GK1 and X1 defends to prevent a goal being scored.

coach's notes

Basically, the art of defending is in keeping opponents playing in front of you and under pressure. Once the player in possession moves behind you or players out of possession move behind opponents in order to be pass receivers, then the alarm-bells should start ringing for the defending team.

This practice allows players to develop their abilities to defend successfully in 1 v 1 situations, or 2 v 2 , 3 v 3 as the coach indicates. As the ball is travelling from S to O1 X1 should move quickly into a position between 01 and the goal he is attacking and if possible to a position within 3 - 4 yards of O1. Certainly X1 should move into position between O1 and the goal so that he could possibly intercept or block the any attempt at goal by O1. Once O1 has possession, X1 should attempt to move within 2 - 3 yards of the ball and have the "desire" to defend - a great quality in all successful defenders! X1 should watch the ball, make no attempts to tackle for the ball unless certain of winning it and be balanced so as to move in any direction quickly. The feet position and body stance adopted by basketball players when defending is similar to that needed by the agile, quick defender in soccer. Containing O1 and if possible controlling the speed and direction in which he moves, should be the aim of X1 while he waits for the chance to either dispossess 01 or block any shots.

The practice can be further extended by allowing two attackers to oppose two defenders and consequently pressurizing, marking and covering can be developed by the coach. Should the defenders win possession of the ball then they should attempt to score past GK2 and the team who lost possession must now recover quickly to defend their own goal.

practice no. 22

Purpose

pressurizing and defending in 1 v 1

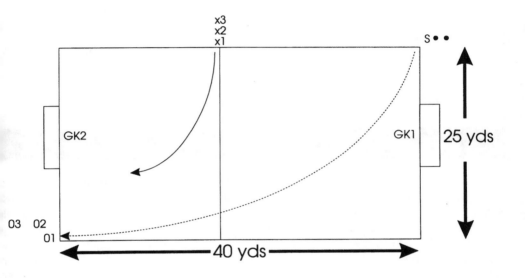

playing area	players involved: - 13
1. 25 yards long x 30 yards wide	1. 1 goalkeeper
	2. 12 outfield players

equipment	practice rules:-
1. 1 goal	1. Players work in pairs, one attacker and one defender.
2. 6 red shirts/bibs	2. Pairs are numbered - 1, 2, 3 etc.
3. 6 white shirts/bibs	3. Coach serves the ball. On calling out a number, two players oppose each other in 1 v 1, 2 v 2 situations etc.

coach's notes

When defending against an opponent who has his back to him a defender should attempt to intercept any passes to the attacker if at all possible. Should that be impossible, then the opponent must be marked goal side and closely (within touching distance) as he receives possession. The defender should attempt to 'see' the ball as he defends by crouching low and looking for the ball at the opponent's feet. In this practice the defender can practice defending against his opponent who has his back to him. As the coach calls out the number of the pair of players (attacker and defender) both players should carry the ball quickly out of the playing area past the coach. Should the attacker arrive first then it is likely he will be closely followed by his opponent. The defender should attempt to prevent his opponent from turning to face the goal, but if the attacker does turn then he should defend 1 v 1 as in the previous practice to prevent his opponent from scoring.

The coach may further extend the practice by calling out two or three numbers together, so that defenders can work in two's or threes against similar numbers of opponents.

practice no. 23

Purpose

defending against opponents with backs to goal

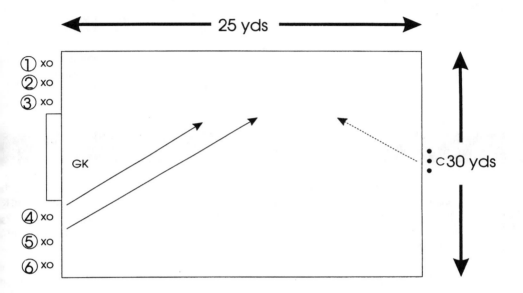

playing area	players involved: - 18
1. 70 yards long x 50 yards wide	1. 2 teams of 7 v 7
	2. Each team also has a sweeper
	3. 2 goalkeepers
equipment	**practice rules:-**
1. 2 portable goals	1. Free play by all outfield players EXCEPT:-
2. 8 red shirts/bibs	2. Sweeper has a maximum of 3 touches on any occasion he has possession.
3. 8 white shirts/bibs	3. GK must throw the ball out.
	4. Both teams attempt to mark opponents man-for-man.

coach's notes

Marking opponents is perhaps the most important of all defending skills, especially when allied to defending against an opponent in possession of the ball. Good marking can be observed when defenders can see the ball and their man, are generally between their opponent and the center of their own goal and are in a position where they may intercept any pass to their opponent.

In this practice, players should mark an opponent on a man-for-man basis and attempt to prevent him from receiving a pass or be in a position to 'pressurize' should he receive the ball. Both sweepers have the freedom to operate unopposed and can therefore direct the play of their team.

Players must learn to concentrate when marking their opponents as clever attackers are very adept at profiting from a defender's lapse of concentration and marking discipline. Marking should be relatively close if opponents are within short passing distance from the man in possession. 'Marking' within 1 - 2 yards may be called for so as not to allow opponents the freedom to receive and turn. However, marking may be from a distance of 5 - 6 yards from an opponent when passing range is over a longer distance. So proximity to defenders will change as the position of the ball changes, and marking angles will also change as players move. Above all else, players should develop the concentration, application and discipline to mark their immediate opponent in this practice.

practice no. 24

Purpose
marking opponents

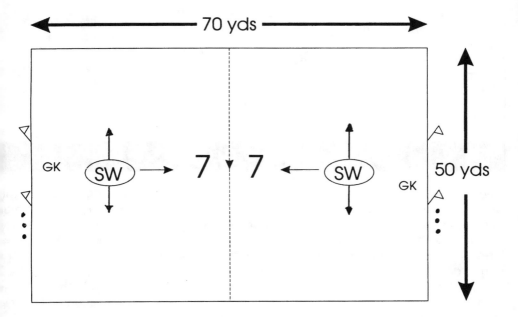

playing area	players involved: - 16
1. Half a soccer field 2. 2 x 5 yards semi-circles around 6 yards wide goals. 3. 1 normal size goal and 6 yards box.	1. 2 teams, each with eight players.

equipment	practice rules:-
1. Two portable goals or corner flags as goal posts. 2. Marker cones to signify goal-area of 2 small goals. 3. Supply of balls around perimeters of the field.	1. Play a free game of 8 v 8. 2. One team to score by shooting, chipping ball through either of 2 small goals. Opponents score in full size goals. 3. There are no goalkeepers and no outfield players allowed into shaded zones.

coach's notes

Good defenders understand about marking, covering and pressurizing duties. In thi
practice, all those defensive fundamentals can be developed. Because of the smal
dimensions of this pitch, a goal could be scored by a player from almost anywhere, i
not directly then certainly within 1 pass. As there are no goalkeepers, players mus
'pressurize' opponents to prevent them passing, shooting or chipping the ball into the
unguarded goals. Consequently, defenders should attempt to move to within 2 -
yards of the man in possession of the ball and prevent the ball moving in the directio
of their goal or goals. Defenders should always be mindful of their position on the fiel
of play and also their relationship to the goal they are protecting.

In this practice, defenders should be encouraged to prevent opponents from playin
the ball directly into their goal. By getting close to the ball and 'in line' with the bal
and the goal they are protecting, they prevent the ball from being immediately deliv
ered into that goal. Marking of likely receivers of passes is a further necessity and 'cov
ering' of teammates vital to understand.

The game can be played for 20 minutes. Each team defends the 'two' goals for 1(
minutes and the 'one' goal for the remaining time. A record of goals scored in any o
the goals can be kept to discover the winner. Here, quick and intelligent pressurizin
accurate marking and selective covering can be encouraged in a single practice.

practice no. 25

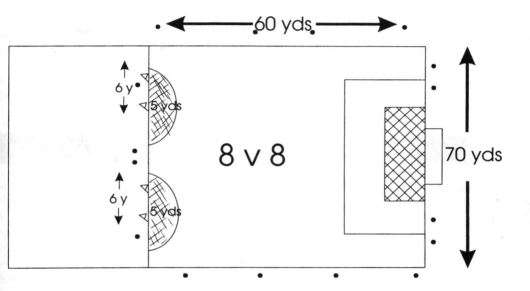

playing area	**players involved: - 16**
1. 50 yards X 30 yards	1. 2 teams of 7 players
	2. 2 goalkeepers

equipment	**practice rules:-**
1. 2 portable goals or 4 corner flags as goals.	1. Ball must be played between teammates in the sequence, of THROW, HEAD, CATCH.
2. Supply of balls around the field.	2. Goals can only be scored by heading the ball into the net.

coach's notes

This practice encourages good heading and passing and movement as a team. One team has possession of the ball and the man in possession is not allowed to run with the ball or carry the ball in any manner. He must throw the ball to a team-mate who must head the ball, so the sequence carried out so far is throw, head. The next player must catch the ball before throwing it to a teammate. Consequently the team in possession makes progress by throwing, heading, catching and throwing again. Should the ball come to the ground, the first player on the scene should pick it up and commence the sequence. Opponents may intercept the ball any way they choose head or hands, but not feet. Throw-ins are awarded should the ball leave the pitch but no corners. If the team concedes three corners it counts as one goal against them. The game allows all kinds of heading to be practiced and is a free-moving, exciting game. It is suitable for a warm-up exercise as well as a game in its own right.

practice no. 26

Purpose
heading

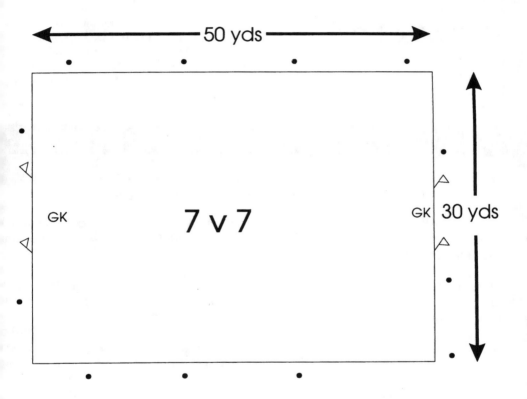

50 yds

7 v 7

GK   GK   30 yds

playing area	**players involved: - 17**
1. 44 yards X 18 yards wide (penalty area)	1. Two wingers each side of the penalty box.
2. Target area for the delivery of crosses marked ▨▨▨▨▨	2. 1 goalkeeper
	3. 6 attackers each side of semi-circle.
equipment	**practice rules:-**
1. 1 goal	1. 'W' plays the ball forward 5 yards and crosses into penalty box.
2. Plentiful supply of balls.	2. As winger touches ball forward, 2 attackers break into the goal-scoring area from their cone and head to score past the goalkeeper.
3. 2 marker cones	

coach's notes

This practice involves a winger crossing the ball with quality into the goal-scoring area for attackers to attempt to score by heading the ball past the goalkeeper.

The winger on playing the ball forward should look into the goal-scoring area and deliver his cross outside the reach of the goalkeeper attempting to play the ball into the area at head-height for the strikers.

The strikers should, on seeing the crosser play the ball forward, break from their marker cone and attack the near-post and center-goal areas along the edge of the 6 yard box. On contacting the ball, a striker should attempt to keep his header low and head the ball down if possible, using his forehead to do so. He may have to dive forward to head the ball as this is frequently required in goal scoring situations. An attacker should be ever alert for rebounds from the goalkeeper and should attempt to make contact with the ball arriving in the goal-scoring area. Too often, strikers do not do all they can to make contact with crosses and so a goal-scoring chance is lost. While the practice is designed for strikers to head for goal, the service may not be as accurate as the coach intends. Consequently strikers should be aware of the necessity to score, using any skill - volleys, half-volleys, overhead scissor-kick, control, turn and shoot - striker should be prepared to score, anytime, anywhere, **anyhow!**

One practice guideline - have left footed players cross the ball from the left side and right footed players from the right for a more assured service.

practice no. 27

Purpose
heading to score

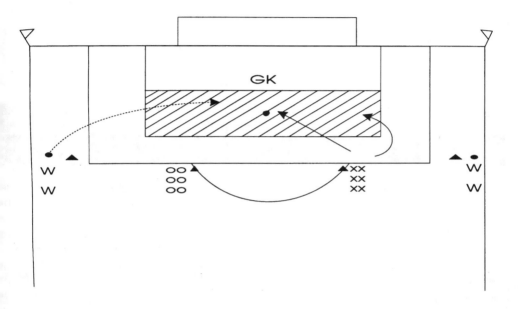

playing area	**players involved: - 8**
1. 44 yards X 36 yards (double penalty area)	1. 2 goalkeepers 2. 4 servers 3. 2 rebound players
equipment 1. Portable goals 2. Supply of balls.	**practice rules:-** 1. (S) within 3 touches shoots at GK from not closer than 18 yards. 2. (R) - rebounding players follow shots in at goal to score from mishandling.

coach's notes

Goalkeepers seem to receive regular training in technique development but very little in the positional aspects of their trade. Positioning the goalkeeper to use his techniques is a vital role of a coach. In this practice, as GK1 serves/rolls the ball to S1, GK2 must position himself correctly to employ his shot-stopping techniques. He should move to his right and into a position that enables him to move equidistant to cover a shot entering his goal at either side. His position would therefore be nearer to his right hand post the more S1 moves to his left. As well as moving sideways to be in position, the goalkeeper should also advance off his goal-line approximately 4 -5 yards towards the ball. By doing this he actually has slightly less distance to move to prevent any shot entering inside the posts. This is known as "narrowing the angle." Once he has moved quickly into position according to the movement of the ball, he should be ready to move to save any shot. Hit feet should be approximately shoulder width apart, his knees slightly bent and head and chest slightly ahead of his feet. Hands should be just in front of his body with palms facing the ball and his weight on the balls of his feet. He should react to shots and not anticipate shots and obviously where possible should secure possession of the ball rather than knocking the ball down or out towards opponents in the penalty area.

practice no. 28

<u>**Purpose**</u>
goalkeeping:- shot-stopping and positioning

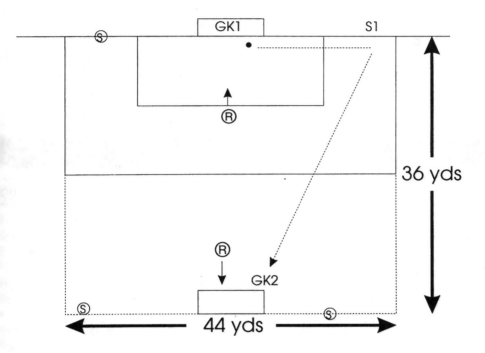

playing area 1. 44 yards x 36 yards 　(double penalty area)	**players involved: - 8** 1. 2 teams of 6 players 2. 2 goalkeepers
equipment 1. 6 red shirts/bibs 2. 6 white shirts/bibs 3. 2 portable goals 4. Supply of balls.	**practice rules:-** 1. GK distributes to any of his team in the rear half of the playing area. 2. Play 4 v 2 to create chance to shoot at the goalkeeper of the opposition. 3. Two players in attacking half rebound shots at the goalkeeper, and may also receive passes in order to shoot.

coach's notes

Following the previous practice, a goalkeeper needs to develop his skills of positioning and shot-stopping in a more challenging, game-type practice. Here, the goalkeeper must continually readjust his position to face up to attackers who are in possession and may be constantly changing position. The GK should move according to the movement of the ball, always remembering to position himself equidistant from the two posts (regardless of the location of the man in possession of the ball O) and approximately 4 - 5 yards off his goal-line, he should move quickly into position taking care to balance himself as he does so and also avoid crossing his legs as he moves. Unless he has to sprint quickly, his feet should move together from side to side and should 'brush' the surface of the pitch in doing so. On making saves, the goalkeeper must be aware of two strikers following up any shots that he mishandles. If he cannot 'hold' the ball when making a save, he should deflect the ball out of play. On gaining possession the goalkeeper should quickly attempt to distribute the ball accurately to a team-member and adjust his position once again.

practice no. 29

Purpose

goalkeeping:- shot-stopping and positioning
(opposite practice)

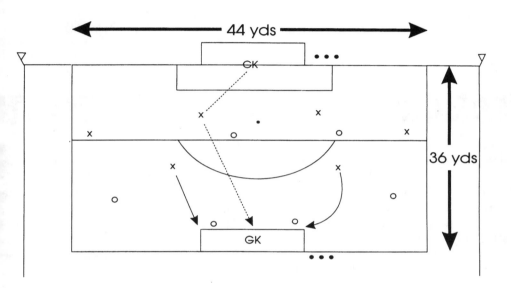

playing area	players involved: - 4
1. Approximately half of the soccer field	1. 2 goalkeepers
2. Field width 44 yards and two 10 yard channels for the wingers.	2. 2 wingers
equipment	**practice rules:-**
1. Marker cones laid down as illustrated.	1. GK 1 throws ball to W1
2. Supply of balls in each goal.	2. W1, within 3 touches, crosses ball long and high into penalty area for GK2 to collect.
	3. Distribute to W2 to cross for GK1.

coach's notes

Goalkeepers must be able to act positively and safely on the ball being crossed into the penalty box by the opposition. The goalkeeper can be a dominating influence in his penalty box or he van be a liability! Three important factors will dominate his ability to handle crossing situations, 1) Positioning 2) Judgement 3) Action (to attack the cross or not). His position will vary according to the angle and distance of the cross. For long range crosses (i.e. from positions wide of the penalty box and in the attacking third of the field), his positioning should be just backward of central between his posts, with his front foot on an imaginary center line drawn out from his goal. He should be 2 - 3 yards off his goal-line so that he can increase the range to which he can move out of goal to attack any cross. From this distance, it is unlikely that any cross would travel directly into his goal from the crosser as he has time to move to cover any such attempt. From his position the goalkeeper should 'open' up his body slightly out from his goal. By 'opening up' his body, the goalkeeper would appear to be positioning his body with his back to the crowd behind his goal. From this position he can assess the situation in and around his penalty area and give information to his fellow players. He can also judge the flight of the cross but he must NOT anticipate the direction and target area for the cross.

He should wait until the cross has been delivered and quickly decide whether to attack the cross or advise his defenders to attack it. If he chooses to deal with the cross he may have to wait and judge when he can catch the ball at the highest point of his one-footed jump. He must also decide whether to catch the cross or to punch high and wide to safety, attempting to clear the penalty area with the punch if possible.

Goalkeepers need much practice on positioning and decision making on crosses coming into the penalty box. This practice is simply organized and allows the goalkeeper to practice everything mentioned above. The winger can also be instructed to vary the distance and type of cross as well as sometimes crossing from the bye-line or areas along the sides of the penalty box.

practice no. 30

Purpose
goalkeeping:- handling crosses

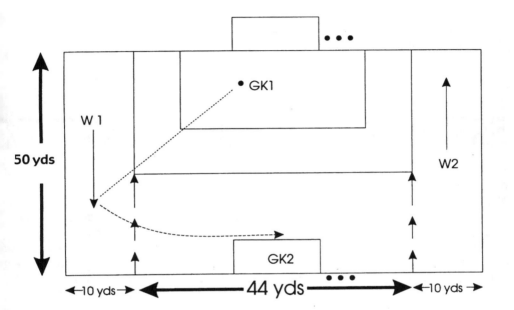

playing area	players involved: - 12
1. Half the field - 60 yards 2. 44 yards WIDE CHANNEL over the length of the field. 3. Half the field divided into two halves of 30 yards each.	1. 2 goalkeepers 2. 2 wingers 3. 4 defenders 4. 4 attackers
equipment	**practice rules:-**
1. Shirts/bibs to distinguish attackers and defenders. 2. Marker cones laid down as illustrated to mark channel and half-way lines. 3. Supply of balls behind the goal.	1. Players remain in zones 2. GK delivers to W or to A1 and A2 3. A/A2 passes wide to W 4. W crosses the ball within 3 touches.

coach's notes

The test of any goalkeeper's ability to deal with crosses is for him to operate under pressure from opponents being marked by his own defenders. His positioning principles do not change from those detailed in the previous practice as the ball and the goal are his two main locating guidelines. However, before the cross is delivered in this practice, he must remind his defenders of their marking responsibilities as well as taking up a correct position. He must also decide whether he can attack the cross or advise his defenders to challenge. In taking the latter course, he should give them clear information to attack the cross, shouting clearly and loudly "AWAY!!" and readjust his own position according to the flight, direction and distance of the ball. He may also have to make a save from a strike by an opponent so he should change his position and stay alert. If the goalkeeper decides to attack the cross, he should shout loudly and early 'KEEPER'S BALL.' He must be certain of making contact with the ball and should make his decision to do so as early as possible, even though he may have to wait to attack the cross. By communicating early to his defenders, they can take action by possibly dropping to cover the space behind the goalkeeper, between him and his goal-line, or even drop quickly onto the goal-line. If the goalkeeper catches the ball he should quickly secure its safe possession in his hands or arms and immediately look for an open receiver for a throw or kick that may launch a counter-attack. If he punches the ball, he should quickly recover back towards his goal, positioning himself for a strike at goal from any opponent. In this practice, two goalkeepers can work and develop their understanding and responsibilities on crosses delivered into the penalty box.

practice no. 31

Purpose
goalkeeping:- crosses

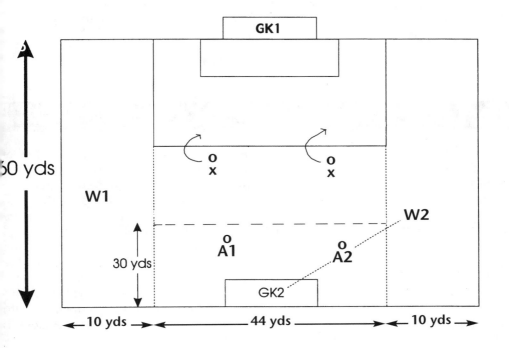

playing area	players involved: - 8
1. Penalty area extended 10 yards	1. 1 goalkeeper
	2. 1 server
	3. 6 attacking players
equipment	**practice rules:-**
1. Marker cones - placed 5 yards apart as indicated.	1. (S) - play balls to X1 or X2
2. Supply of balls.	2. X1 runs with the ball through cones and at the goalkeeper.
	3. Score past the GK in 1 v 1
	a. shoot
	b. dribble past GK

coach's notes

A testing situation for any goalkeeper is to be faced by an oncoming attacker, free of opposition, which amounts to a 1 v 1 confrontation between the two players. The goalkeeper must act intelligently and carefully, doing nothing that could help the attacker to beat the goalkeeper easily. As the attacker approaches the goal, the goalkeeper should come forward from his position on his goal-area line (6 yards). He should move slowly forward taking 'shuffling' small steps to do so, so that he is always balanced to dive or react quickly if he is required to. If he advances too far forward too quickly he may be "chipped" by the attacking player. He must in effect narrow the angle, remaining equidistant between his two posts, moving forward slowly as he does so, his weight should be balanced so as to move quickly. His knees will be bent slightly, his body bent at the hips and his head forward, bringing his weight forward onto the balls of his feet. His hands should be around waist height with his elbows close to his body. From this position he is physically ready to act, but he must be mentally aggressive and wanting to win what could be a battle of wits. The goalkeeper should concentrate on the ball and not be deceived by any feints by the attacker in possession. He should be looking for the opportunity to attack the ball should the attacker push it too far out of his feet and therefore lose control. Consequently the goalkeeper should concentrate and wait for this possibility. Should the attacker not offer this opportunity then he can do one of two things. He may shoot or attempt to dribble past the goalkeeper. Should he attempt to shoot then as in all situations the goalkeeper should react quickly to the shot and not anticipate before the shot is taken, otherwise he would "sell" himself and make the attacker's problem much easier. If the striker attempts to dribble, the goalkeeper again should look for the opportunity to attack the ball quickly should the striker push the ball too far forward or to the side and so lose control. On moving for the ball the goalkeeper should attack it if possible with his hands and either smother it or push the ball away out of the striker's control while he recovers to his feet as quickly as possible, either to further attack the ball or to recover to a new position to counter another attack at goal.

practice no. 32

Purpose
goalkeeping:- 1 v 1 against attacking player

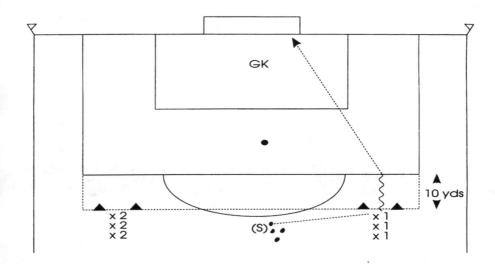

playing area	**players involved: - 8**
1. 45 yards x 44 yards wide	1. 2 teams of 6
	2. 2 neutral players
	3. 1 goalkeeper
equipment	**practice rules:-**
1. 6 red shirts/bibs	1. GK1 feeds the ball to any player on his team.
2. 6 white shirts/bibs	2. They play against three opponents to pass the ball to their 3 attackers or neutral players in the attacking half.
3. 2 neutral shirts	
4. 2 portable goals	3. Play to score
5. Supply of balls	4. Players initially remain in their own half of the field.
	5. For good players, limit the play to 2 touch.

coach's notes

A practice that embodies everything concerning good soccer - passing, movement, finishing and individual ability. Both neutral players play for whichever team has possession, they never defend. Players in this practice should learn to see as much of the playing area as possible and to know the situation in which they are playing - I call it "AWARENESS." Awareness means looking away from the ball and seeing positions to take-up, knowing where opponents are so that should you receive a pass you are aware of their proximity and can play accordingly.

Players can combine together to make wall-passes possible, can receive and turn to shoot, dribble and many attacking skills can be developed. By limiting the number of touches per player to 2, quick inter-passing and the development of simple, effective ground passing can be encouraged, as well as quick shooting.

Add two wingers per team who operate outside the playing area, and a crossing and finishing practice can be devised. Scoring with only 1 touch from the cross can be a rule and all types of crosses can be developed and encouraged.

A free-flowing, quick, lively and beneficial practice that can produce a variety of skills and techniques.

practice no. 33

Purpose

passing, movement, goal-scoring

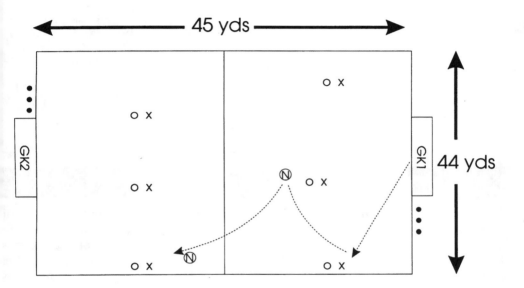

playing area	**players involved: - 18**
1. 70 yards x 50 yards wide	1. 2 teams of 9 a side
equipment 1. 8 red shirts/bibs 2. 8 white shirts/bibs 3. 2 portable goals 4. 2 goalkeeper jerseys	**practice rules:-** 1. Both teams play man-for-man marking of opponents. 2. Both teams have one player nominated as sweeper (free player) who can only play in his defending half and has a maximum 3 touches when in possession of the ball. 3. Goalkeeper must release the ball to his sweeper on gaining possession.

coach's notes

The essence of successful soccer is being superior to your immediate opponent. In this practice all players have the opportunity to develop both attacking and defending skills in 1 v 1 situations. The attacking team being closely marked on a man-to-man basis must work hard at the correct time to change pace and direction to lose their markers in order to receive. Individual and combined movement (i.e. cross-over runs) by attackers may help them to break free. For certain, a lack of movement will make them easy to mark. With the sweeper in possession and ready and able to pass, attackers must time their movements to break free to be a receiver. On receiving the ball they are likely to be opposed by a defender. Consequently they must decide whether to beat the defender in a 1 v 1 situation by dribbling, or to combine with a team-mate possibly by using a wall-pass to eliminate the opponent.

Defenders must mark correctly. They should be goal-side of their opponents, able to see man and ball and have a good chance of intercepting any pass that is made to him, as outlined in PRACTICE NO. 24 earlier in the book. The sweeper can both attack and defend. He must in possession have no more than 3 touches and decide who to pass to and how to pass to him if he is tightly marked. Defensively he must learn how to cover his teammates and when to take over marking responsibilities if a teammate is beaten.

As well as the soccer qualities, players must develop the determination to recover quickly if possession has been lost and mark their opposite number. When marking concentration, alertness and discipline are vital qualities to be successful. A good all-round practice where all skills relative to attacking and defending can be developed.

practice no. 34

Purpose

defending:- man marking
attacking:- losing markers playing 1 v 1

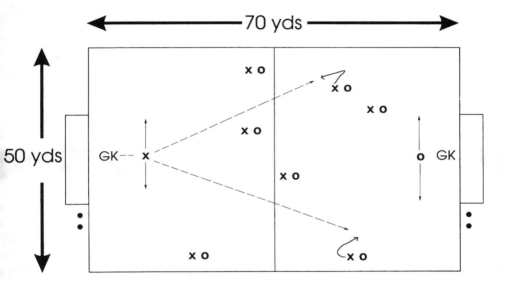

playing area	**players involved: - 18**
1. 50 yards x 40 yards wide	1. 2 teams of 6, -3 attackers and 3 defenders in each team.
	2. 2 goalkeepers
equipment	**practice rules:-**
1. 6 red shirts/bibs	1. Defenders mark man-for-man on attacking opponents.
2. 6 white shirts/bibs	2. GK distributes to any player who is free, especially if in the half nearest to him.
3. 2 goalkeeper jerseys	
4. 2 portable goals - 8 yards wide	3. Players remain in their own half of the field.
5. Supply of balls	

coach's notes

Both defenders and attacking players can develop their individual and combined skill in this practice. Attackers must work to free themselves of their markers in order to receive passes from their own players. On receiving the ball they must determine whether to 'screen' the ball, turn with the ball or possibly combine in an interchange of passes with a colleague in order to score past the goalkeeper. Breaking free of the marker involves a player changing pace and direction quickly and also being aware of the position of the marker on moving to receive the ball.

Defenders can develop their marking and intercepting abilities and must also defend in 1 v 1 situations when their opponent has possession of the ball.

The goalkeeper should try to find a free player in the half nearest to him so that those players can develop their passing ability also. Should that not be possible, then he may throw the ball to his strikers in the attacking half.

Free play should be encouraged in that all players may have as many touches as necessary when in possession. The game can be further developed by allowing one player who has possession in the defending half to either run with the ball (if possible) to play in the attacking half or pass into the attacking half and then move forward to assist his team-mates to outnumber opposition.

practice no. 35

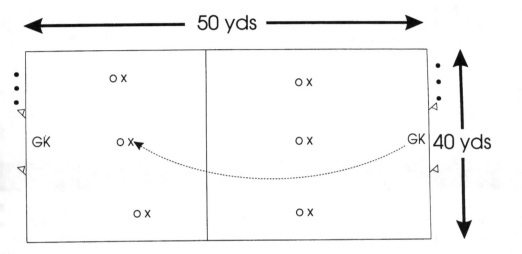

playing area	**players involved: - 18**
1. Half a soccer field 2. 60 yards x 70 yards	1. 2 teams of 6, -3 attackers and 3 defenders in each team. 2. 2 goalkeepers
equipment	**practice rules:-**

1. 3 sets of different colored jersey
2. Supply of balls
3. 4 goals - 10 yards wide -
   (use cones/corner flags etc.)
	1. No player allowed in the 8 yards
	   zone.
	2. 4 (T) target men play in the 10
	   yard goal but behind the line.
	3. 7 v 7 + (3N) play to (T) at one
	   end, receive possession again and
	   play to other end of the field.

coach's notes

Twenty one players can enjoy a worthwhile and enjoyable session using this practice. Teams can play against each other for say a period of ten minutes before the neutral team (4 (T) + 3 N players) replaces them. So each team takes it in turn to be the neutral team who always return the ball to the team who last played it to them. On gaining possession, a team can attack one end and pass from anywhere to a target man (T) behind the end line. The target man must return the ball to the team who passed it to him or to a neutral player who assists the team having possession. On receiving the ball a team must then attack either of the target players positioned between the goals at the other end. Should passes to the target men be inaccurate (they must be controlled by (T)), then a ball is served by (T) to the opposition team.

Plenty of quality passing and thoughtful movement is required to play this game successfully and short and long passes, combined plays and individual play can all be developed in order to successfully pass the ball to a target man.

Players can be allowed freedom of touches or can be restricted to say one or two touches in possession. Should the ball go out of bounds at the sides of the pitch, then a throw-in is awarded as in a normal soccer game.

practice no. 36

Purpose
Possession, support and general attacking play

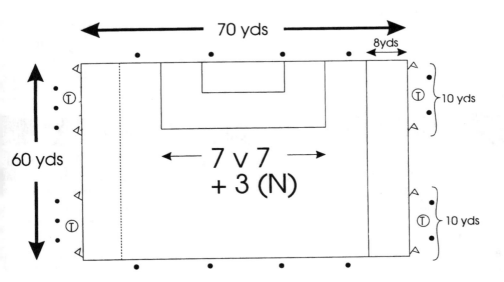

playing area	players involved: - 12
1. 60 yards x 40 yards	1. 6 X's 2. 6 O's

equipment	practice rules:-
1. 6 red shirts/bibs 2. 6 white shirts/bibs 3. Supply of balls	1. Team in possession has 2 touches only. 2. The defending team should gain possession and switch the play to their free player. 3. Team roles then reverse.

coach's notes

All types of passes are involved in this practice. The team in possession (O) has 6 players in one half of the pitch and must play 2 touch soccer. The opponents have 5 players who must attempt to gain possession of the ball. Four players may be used t defend, leaving 2 in the other half of the pitch if player quality is not so good. On having possession, O's should pass the ball quickly and accurately amongst themselves passing and moving as required. On gaining possession the opponents X should deliver a long pass to their free player and move quickly to their own half to support him - X's now have 6 players in their half. On losing possession, 5 O's should move t defend and regain possession in their opponent's half, leaving one target man behind So each team has the opportunity to attack and defend as possession is lost. The player left behind as the 'free' or target man can either be nominated or rotated in turn b simply numbering the players. He should adjust his position continuously in order t make himself a receiver of a pass when his outnumbered team gains possession.

practice no. 37

Purpose

passing, possession and movement

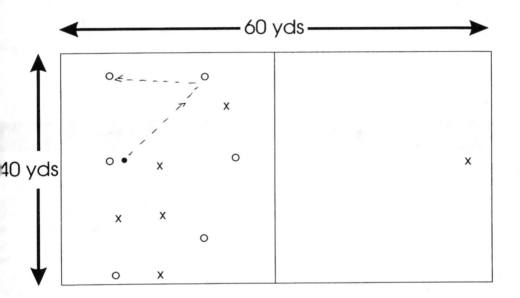

playing area 1. 50 yards x 30 yards	players involved: - 14 1. 2 teams of 7 v 7
equipment 1. 7 red shirts/bibs 2. 7 white shirts/bibs 3. Supply of balls	practice rules:- 1. Team gaining possession keep the ball away from their opponent. 2. Players may be restricted to two touches or can be allowed to play free.

coach's notes

In this practice, two teams play 'keep-away' against each other. In doing so, the coach may encourage different skills to be used. For instance - on gaining possession a challenge may be issued to the team to execute as many wall-passes as possible during their possession. To score 20 consecutive passes can be a further target for a team and one pass over 30 yards can be counted as 3 passes. A rule may also be applied that players should pass the ball in sequence from numbered players one to two to three to four, etc. This will encourage players to move quickly into position to receive a pass from a teammate. A variety of conditions may be placed on the practice for the coach to develop certain skills used in the game. Having at least 5 touches in possession may be a rule, running at least 10 yards when in possession may be another   - encouraging different types of passes may also be a further rule. The coach should not apply rules or demands carelessly but should impose a rule to develop a required skill to be practiced.

practice no. 38

Purpose
General play

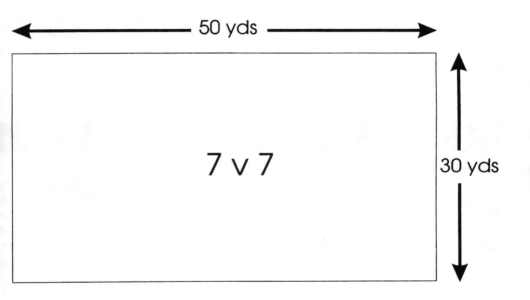

playing area	**players involved: - 15**
1. 60 yards x 40 yards	1. 2 teams of 7
	2. One (or two) goalkeepers

equipment	**practice rules:-**
1. 7 red shirts/bibs	1. Team in possession retain the ball and pass to goalkeeper (who is mobile) whenever possible.
2. 7 white shirts/bibs	2. GK in possession should redistribute the ball to the team from whom he received a pass.
3. Supply of balls	

coach's notes

This is basically a possession practice in that passing, support and movement are th essence of success. The team in possession should attempt to retain possessio through quality passing and support and try to pass the ball into the mobile goa keeper whenever possible. The goalkeeper, in turn, will redistribute the ball to th team having possession and the receiver of his pass can be conditioned to reproduc a certain skill. For example the player must attempt to play a wall-pass, or pass an overlap, or run 10 yards quickly with the ball or perform a particular individual move ment in possession i.e. step over the ball, back heel and turn, etc.

Possibilities are limitless and all the time the coach is seeking to extend the range an quality of player performance. He may indeed give individual tasks - for example, on player may have to pass within 2 touches - another may be asked to execute a wal pass but the coach must know the players' deficiencies and why he is imposing a pa ticular condition on any one player.

This is a multi-faceted practice, very useful as a warm-up practice for senior players an a skill development for youth age performers.

practice no. 39

Purpose
multi-purpose practice

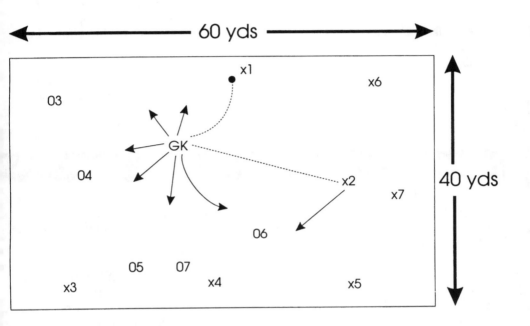

playing area	**players involved: - 15**
1. 60 yards x 40 yards	1. Two teams of seven
	2. 2 goalkeepers
	3. 2 wingers playing for each team

equipment	**practice rules:-**
1. 9 red shirts/bibs	1. Free play within 60 yards x 40
2. 9 white shirts/bibs	yards playing area.
3. 2 goalkeepers jerseys	2. If the ball is passed to wingers out-
4. Portable goals	side the area, he must cross the
3. Supply of balls	ball.
	3. No players except wingers are
	allowed outside the playing area.

coach's notes

A free game of soccer takes place inside the playing area with the intention being to score past the opponent's goalkeeper. However, should a player choose, he may pass the ball to either 'W' in his team. 'W' then must cross the ball for his team and he may cross within 2 touches or may run with the ball to the bye-line before crossing.

Passing, support, movement and crossing and finishing are all included in this practice as are all the qualities necessary for good defending. Conditions may be placed on the practice if needed. Two-touch soccer within the playing area can be imposed crossing the ball within two touches can be imposed on the winger and trying to score by using only one touch can be encouraged from all those striking at goal.

practice no. 40

Purpose

General purpose:- especially crossing and goal-scoring

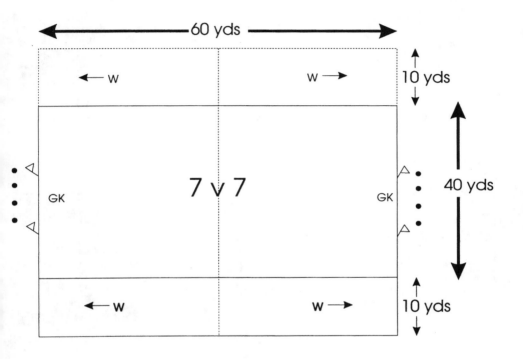

Coaching Books from REEDSWAIN

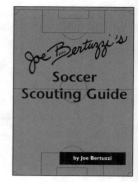

#291
Soccer Fitness Training
by Enrico Arcelli
and Ferretto Ferretti
$12.95

#261
Match Analysis
and Game Preparation
Henny Kormelink and Tjeu Seevrens
$12.95

#789
Soccer Scouting Guide
by Joe Bertuzzi
$12.95

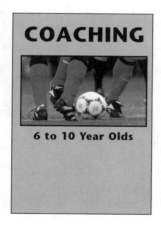

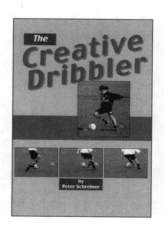

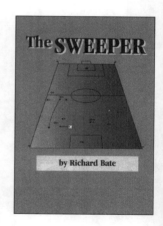

#264
Coaching
6 to 10 Year Olds
by Giuliano Rusca
$14.95

#256
The Creative Dribbler
by Peter Schreiner
$14.95

#225
The Sweeper
by Ricard Bate
$9.95

1-800-331-5191 • www.reedswain.com